Playing With Colour

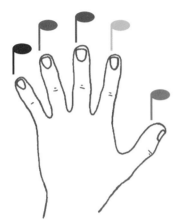

Book 3

Created by Sharon Goodey
www.playingwithcolour.co.uk

Copyright © MMXIII by Alfred Publishing Co (UK) Ltd
All Rights Reserved. Printed in the UK
ISBN: 9781905734023
www.alfredUK.com

Cover design by Wesley Mitchell

Activity Page

The names of the TREBLE SPACES spell FACE.

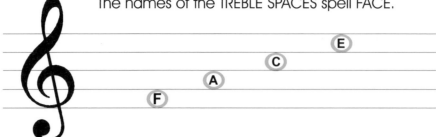

With one finger play and name each of these notes.

The names of the lines are EGBDF. If you practise saying these letters you will find they are quite easy to learn.

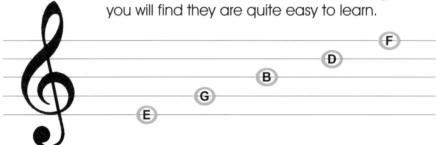

With one finger play and name each of these notes.

Write the names of the following notes.

Do you recognise these two notes?

NOTE READING:

Look for patterns and work out how this will sound before before you play.
Circle an interval of a 3rd.
In the red box write the letter name of the first note.

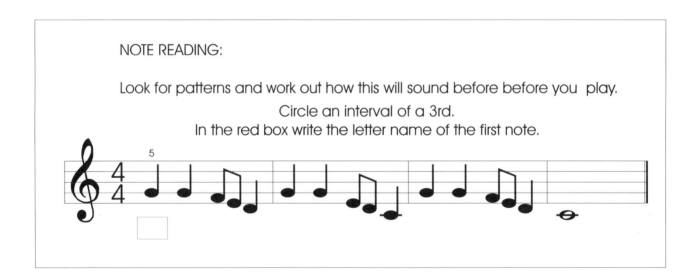

The Warrior Chief

What intervals are played
by the left hand in bar 2: 5th & 2nd

Activity Page

The BASS spaces also spell FACE, but you must
remember to begin below line 1.

With one finger play and name each of these notes.

The names of the lines are EGBDF,
when you begin with the line below line 1.

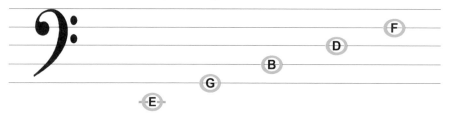

With one finger play and name each of these notes.

Write the letter names of these notes.

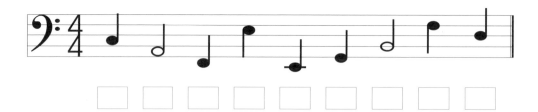

NOTE READING:

Look for patterns and work out how this will sound before before you play.

Circle an interval of a 3rd.
In the red box write the letter name of the first note.

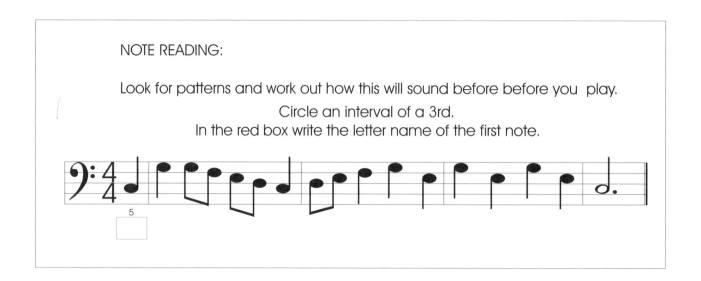

4

Nothing-at-all

In the red boxes write the letter name of the note above.

Activity Page

When you can say these letters easily from memory you can put both sets of letters together so that one follows on from the other.

E G B D F

F A C E

E G B D F

With one finger play and name each of these notes.

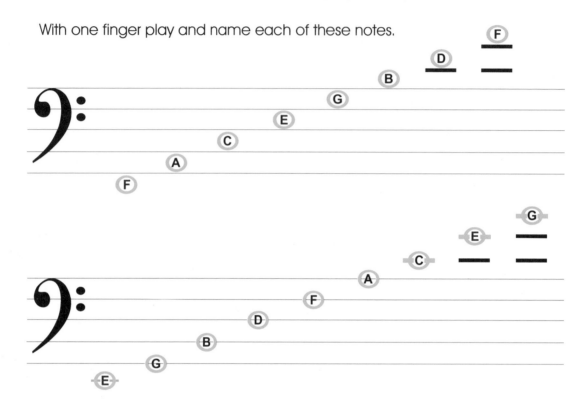

Write the names of the following notes.

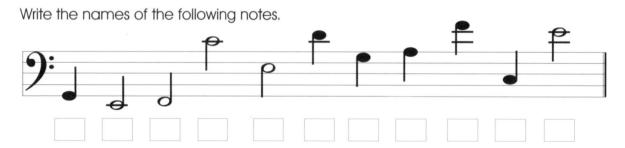

NOTE READING:

Look for patterns and work out how this will sound before before you play.

Circle an interval of a 5th.
In the red box write the letter name of the first note.

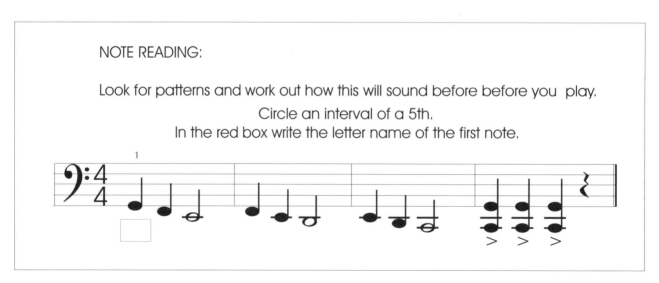

6

Gabriel's Christmas Stomp

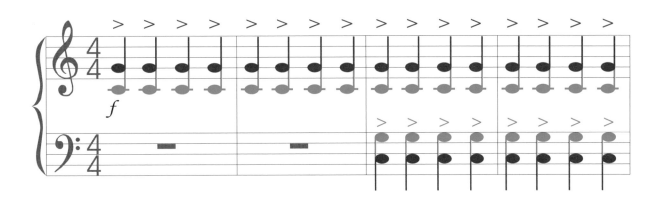

Left hand

Play exactly the same notes now with your right hand

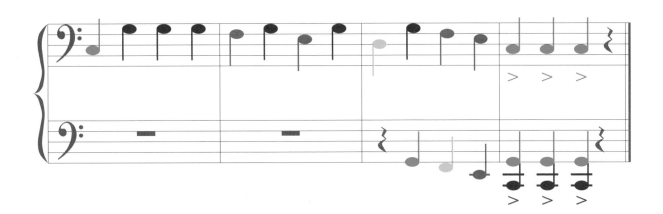

How many **Bass Clefs** can you see in Gabriel's Christmas Stomp?

——

How many **Treble Clefs**?

——

Which clef tells us to play below **Middle C**?

Treble Clef ☐

Bass Clef ☐

Tick the correct box.

There's a Big Ship Sailing

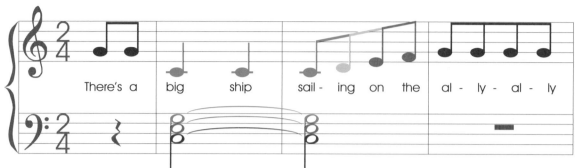

There's a big ship sail - ing on the al - ly - al - ly

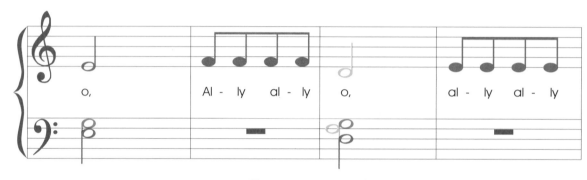

o, Al - ly al - ly o, al - ly al - ly

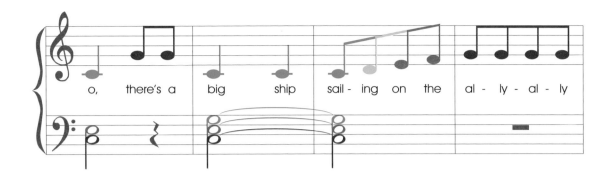

o, there's a   big   ship   sail - ing   on   the   al - ly - al - ly

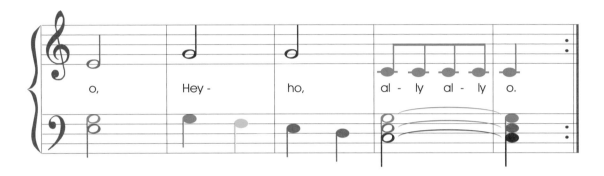

o,   Hey -   ho,   al - ly   al - ly   o.

2. There's a big ship sail-ing and rocking on the sea,
    Rocking on the sea, rocking on the sea,
    There's a big ship sail-ing and rocking on the sea,
    Hay, ho, al-ly al-ly o.

3. The captain said, "It'll never , never do,
    Never, never do, never, never do."
    The captain said, "It'll never, never do,
    Hay, ho, never, never do."

4. The big ship sank to the bottom of the sea,
    Bottom of the sea, bottom of the sea,
    The big ship sank to the bottom of the sea,
    Hay, ho, bottom of thesea."

THE KEY OF C MAJOR:

If we play all the white notes from C to C as shown below we call this the SCALE of C MAJOR.
Learning to play scales helps us to understand patterns in music.
Practise playing the scales below until you can play them easily from memory.

There's a Big Ship Sailing is written using the notes of C major.
It is therefore in the **KEY of C major**.

Practise your sight-reading by
playing this with each hand separately.
When playing with both hands
it may help to write in some
finger numbers.

Nov 20th

London Bridge

Traditional
Arr. by S.G

Look carefully at the hand position before you begin.

Lon - don bridge is | fall - ing down, | fall - ing down, | fall - ing down.

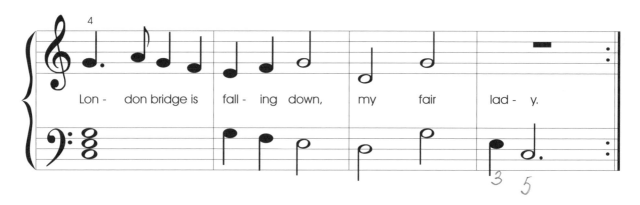

Lon - don bridge is | fall - ing down, | my fair | lad - y.

2 We must build it up again,
   Up again, up again.
   We must build it up again,
   My fair lady.

3 Build it up with wood and clay,
   Wood and clay, wood and clay.
   Build it up with wood and clay,
   My fair lady.

4 Wood and clay will wash away,
   Wash away, wash away.
   Wood and clay will wash away,
   My fair lady.

5 Build it up with stone so strong,
   Stone so strong, stone so strong.
   Build it up with stone so strong,
   My fair lady.

6 Stone so strong will last so long,
   Last so long, last so long.
   Stone so strong will last so long,
   My fair lady.

If we make the 3rd note of a MAJOR key flat
it changes the character of a piece and
makes it sound sad or more thoughtful.
Listen to the difference in this piece when you play the E flats.
We call these kinds of keys MINOR.

Collecting Conkers

The Train Journey

Allegro : quick and lively

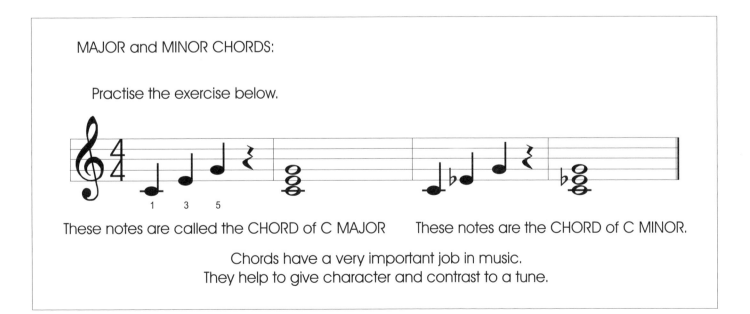

MAJOR and MINOR CHORDS:

Practise the exercise below.

These notes are called the CHORD of C MAJOR   These notes are the CHORD of C MINOR.

Chords have a very important job in music.
They help to give character and contrast to a tune.

Activity Page

The next piece is written in the **KEY of G MAJOR**.
If you play the white notes from G to G, in order for the notes to sound bright and happy, as C major does, you will need to play the F as a sharp.
Try playing these notes with the F sharp and then play them again with an F natural.
Listen to the difference.

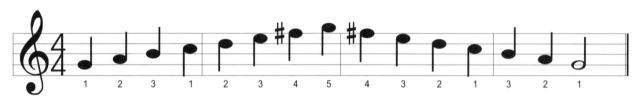

Practise the chord exercise below.

These notes are the CHORD of G MAJOR   These notes are the CHORD of _____

KEY SIGNATURES:

This **Key Signature** tells us that the piece is written in G major and so we must play every F as a sharp.

14

Melody in G

Eberhard Muller
1767-1817

Andante : walking pace

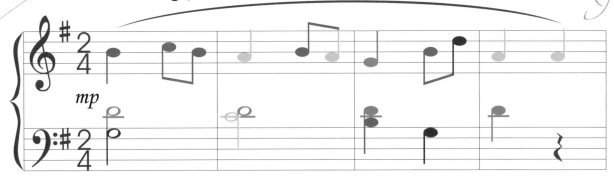

Look carefully at the hand position before you begin.

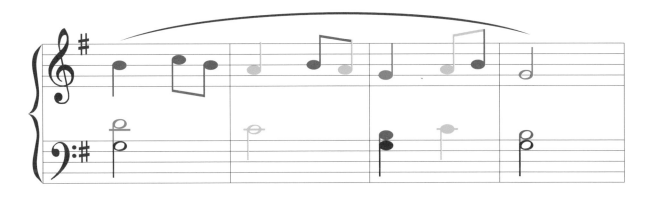

Look carefully here!

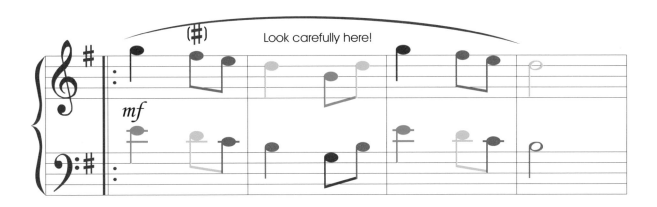

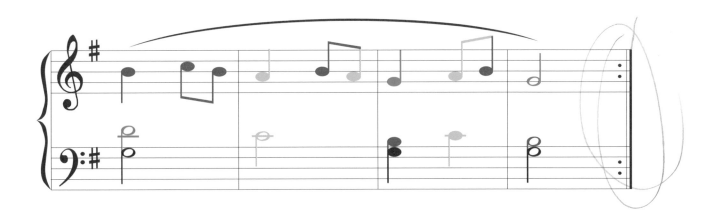

Aiken Drum

Name the notes shown.

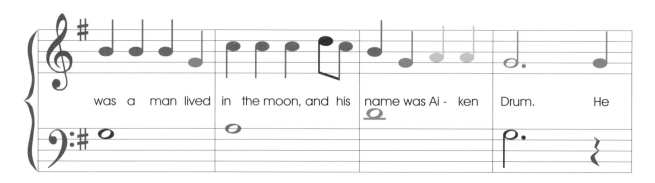

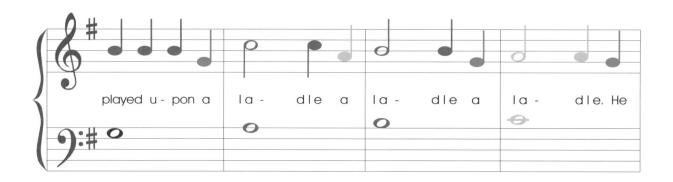

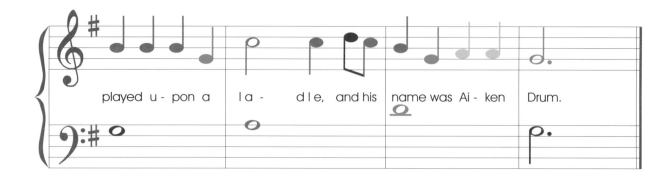

2. His hat was made of good cream cheese,of good cream cheese of good cream cheese.
   His hat was made of good cream cheese, and his name was Aiken Drum.
   He played upon a ladle, a ladle, a ladle.
   He played upon a ladle and his name was Aiken Drum.

3. His coat was made of good roast beef, of good roast beef, of good roast beef.
   His coat was made of good roast beef, and his name was Aiken Drum.
   He played upon a ladle, a ladle, a ladle.
   He played upon a ladle and his name was Aiken Drum.

4. His buttons were made of penny loaves, of penny loaves, of penny loaves,
   His buttons were made of penny loaves, and his name was Aiken Drum.
   He played upon a ladle, a ladle, a ladle,
   He played upon a ladle and his name was Aiken Drum.

5. His breaches made of haggis bags, of haggis bags, of haggis bags.
   His breaches made of haggis bags, and his name was Aiken Drum.
   He played upon a ladle, a ladle, a ladle.
   He played upon a ladle and his name was Aiken Drum.

This song was probably inspired by a story written by William Nicholson 1782-1849 who was born in Dumfries.
The story was called 'Aiken Drum - The Brownie Of Bladnoch'.
The story describes a man who was initially shunned by villagers due to his appearance.
He was eventually accepted and respected as a result of his hard work in the fields and farmlands of the village.
However, he only worked after sunset, by the light of the moon and the stars.
A brownie was a person who worked only for food, hence the references to his clothes being made of food.

Santa is on his Way!

In this piece you will need to use the **sustaining pedal.** This is usually shown by the abbreviation *Ped.*

Allegretto : fairly fast and lively

Pass left hand over right hand

Improvise, following the given rhythm and suggested notes.

The pattern of notes in the last four bars is called a **Broken Chord**. Practise these notes until you can play them from memory.

Write the letter names in the red boxes and look for patterns in the notes and in the letter names.

19

Practise your sight-reading by playing this with each hand separately. When playing with both hands it may help to write in some finger numbers.

Jan. 21st.

Dec 11th.

We Three Kings

John Hopkins Jn 1857

We three kings of O- ri- ent are, Bear - ing

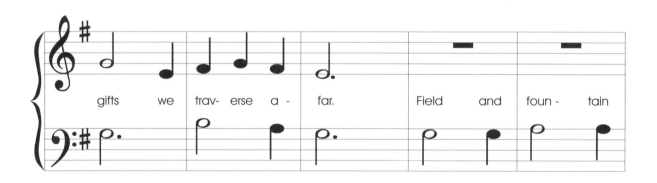

gifts we trav- erse a- far. Field and foun - tain

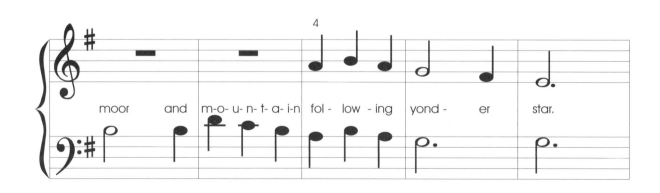

moor and m-o- u- n- t- a-i-n fol - low- ing yond- er star.

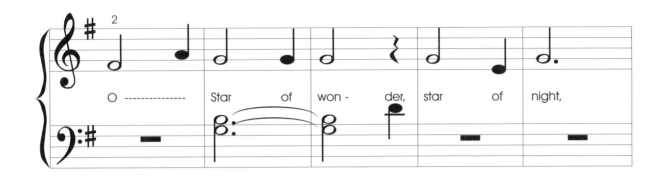

O ---------------- Star of won - der, star of night,

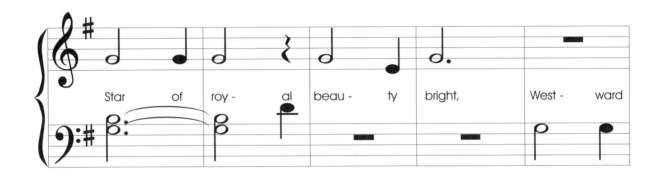

Star of roy - al beau - ty bright, West - ward

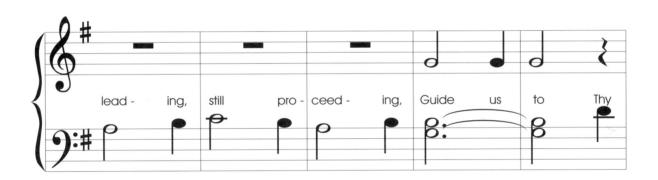

lead - ing, still pro - ceed - ing, Guide us to Thy

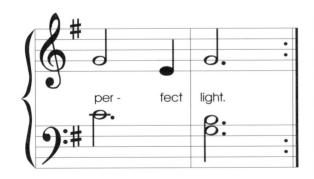

per - fect light.

What is the key of We Three Kings?

_____ major.

How many beats are there in a bar?

_____

Feb 11th.

THE KEY OF F MAJOR:

Silver Moon is written in the key of **F MAJOR**. You will need to play every B as a flat.
Practise the following F major scales.
Look carefully at the right hand fingering.

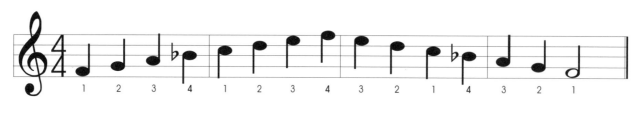

Left hand can be played an octave higher

Practise the chord exercises below.

These notes are the CHORD of ___ MAJOR   These notes are the CHORD of _____

Practise the Broken Chord of F Major.

Silver Moon

Andante : walking pace

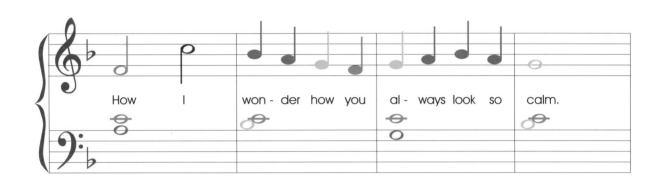

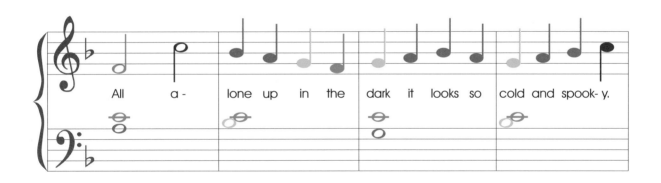

Do Your Ears Hang Low?

Traditional
Arr. by S.G

Feb 11 th.
Feb 25 th

Do your ears hang low? Do they wob- ble to and fro? Can you tie 'em in a knot? Can you

(♮)

tie 'em in a bow? Can you throw 'em o'er your shoulder like a Con - ti - nen - tal soldier? Do your

ears hang low?

How many natural signs
can you see in
this piece?

_____

24

2. Do your ears stick out?
   Can you waggle them about?
   Can you flop 'em up and down as you fly around the town?
   Can you shut them up for sure when you hear an awful bore?
   Do your ears stick out?

3. Do your ears flip flop?
   Can you use 'em as a mop?
   Are they stringy at the bottom?
   Are they curly at the top?
   Can you use 'em for a swatter?
   Can you use 'em for a blotter?
   Do your ears flip flop?

4. Do your ears stand high?
   Do they reach up to the sky?
   Do they hang down when they're wet?
   Do they stand up when they're dry?
   Can you semaphore your neighbour with a minimum of labour?
   Do your ears stand high?

25

Activity Page

NOTE READING:

Reading 5ths and 3rds.
5ths and 3rds are easy to spot because they both move from a
line to a line
or
a space to a space.
Can you see the difference between the 3rds and the 5ths?

Listen carefully to the sound of each **interval**.

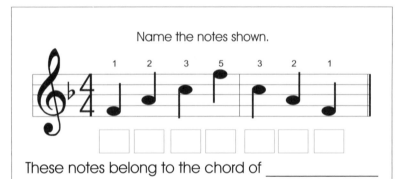

Name the notes shown.

These notes belong to the chord of _____

This pattern of notes is called an arpeggio.

How many times do you play
an arpeggio in
The Wize Old Wizard?

_____

Draw lines between all circles
that have the same value.

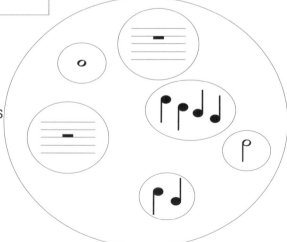

The Wise Old Wizard

Feb 25th

Clap this rhythm before you play

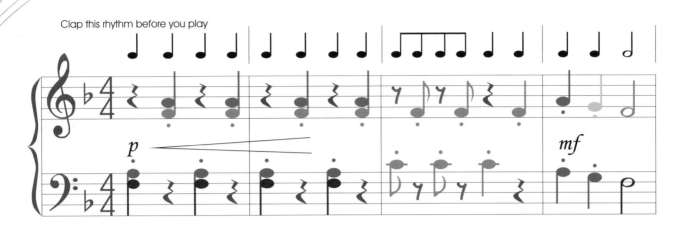

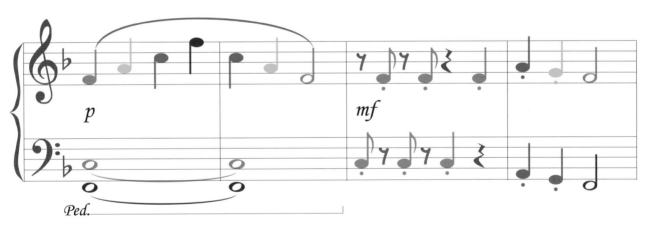

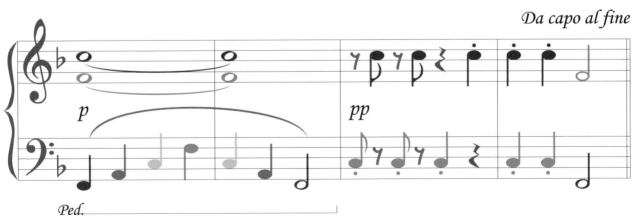

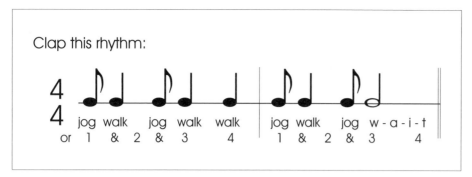

4/4 jog walk jog walk walk | jog walk jog w-a-i-t
or 1 & 2 & 3 4 | 1 & 2 & 3 4

Tossing Pancakes

3ʳᵈ March

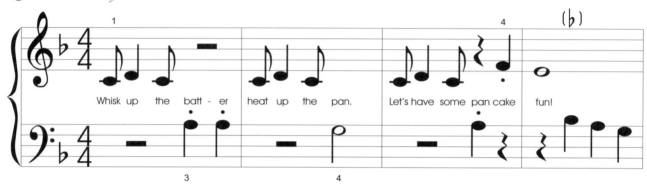

Whisk up the batt-er | heat up the pan. | Let's have some pan cake | fun!

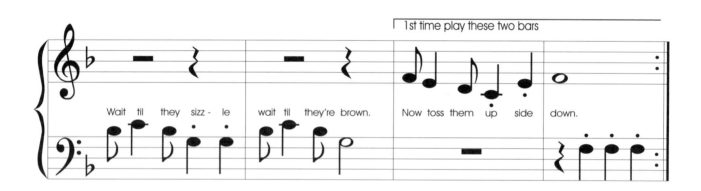

Wait til they sizz-le | wait til they're brown. | Now toss them up side | down.

1st time play these two bars

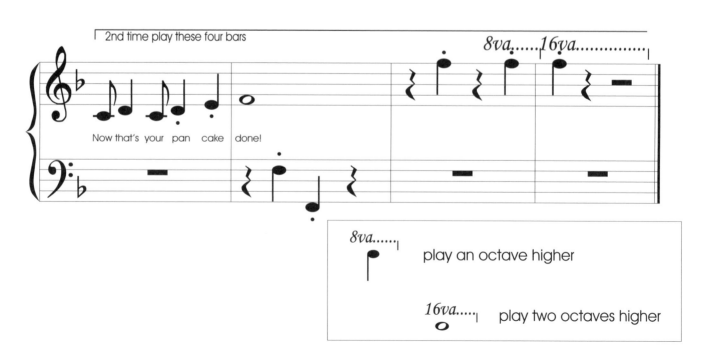

2nd time play these four bars

Now that's your pan cake | done!

8va...... 16va...............

8va......   play an octave higher

16va.....   play two octaves higher

28

Jingle Bells

Clap this rhythm before you play

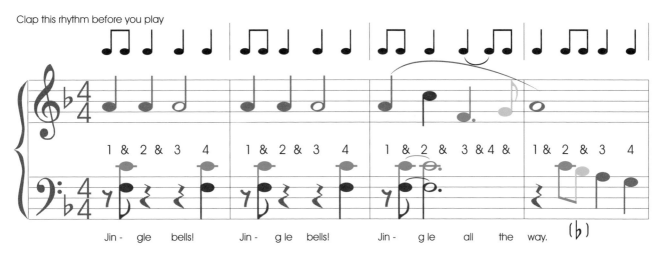

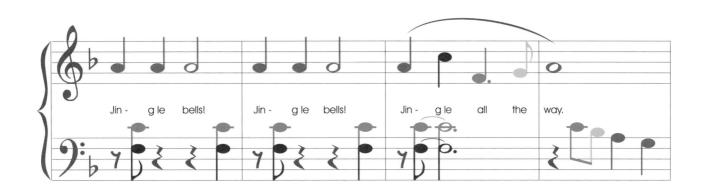

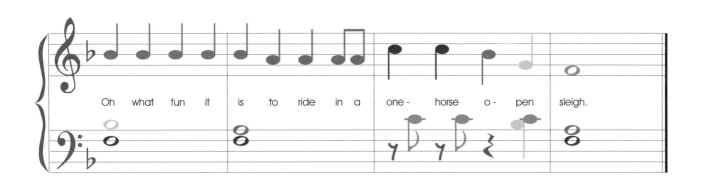

THE KEY OF D MAJOR:

To play in the key of **D MAJOR** you will need to play every F and C as a sharp.
Look carefully at the following two scales.
Practise the scales below until you can play them from memory.

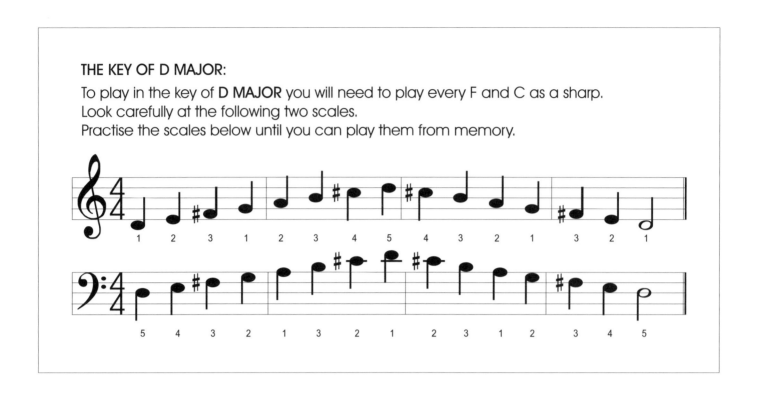

Kum Ba Yah

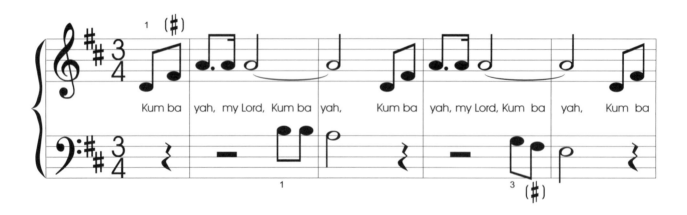

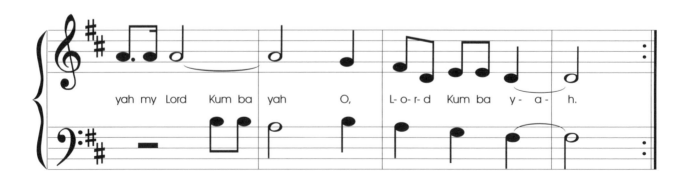

He's Got the Whole World

Traditional
Arr. by S.G

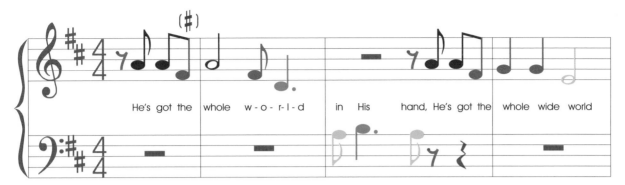

He's got the whole w-o-r-l-d in His hand, He's got the whole wide world

in His hand, He's got the whole w-o-r-l-d in His hand, He's got the

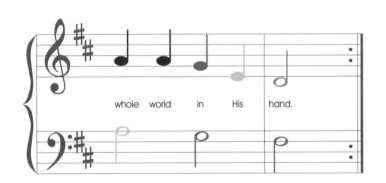

whole world in His hand.

How many quavers (eighth notes) can you count in this piece?

_____

How many quaver (eighth note) rests?

_____

Practise the chord exercises below.

1 3 5

These notes are the CHORD of _____ MAJOR   These notes are the CHORD of _____

Now memorise the Broken Chord of D Minor.

1 3 5   1 2 5   1 3 5   3

31

Ten Green Bottles

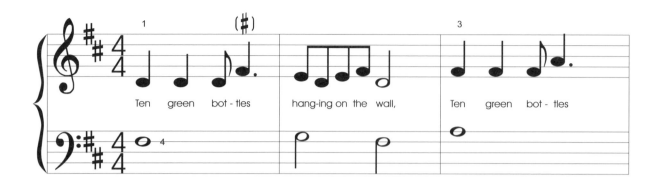

Ten green bot-tles hang-ing on the wall, Ten green bot-tles

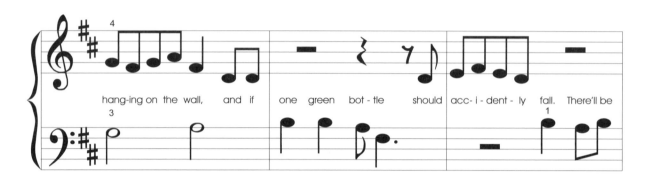

hang-ing on the wall, and if one green bot-tle should acc-i-dent-ly fall. There'll be

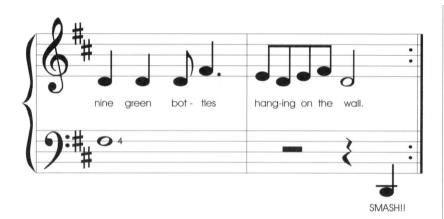

nine green bot-tles hang-ing on the wall.

SMASH!!

The name of the
last note played by the
left hand is ____

This note is a

treble note ☐

bass note ☐

Tick the correct box.

Teddy Bear Waltz

Allegretto : fairly fast and lively

Fine

Improvise, using the **chord of D major** and the given rhythm.

Da capo al fine

Improvise, using the **chord of D major** and the given rhythm.

Activity Page

MINOR KEY SIGNATURES:

'C' MAJOR and 'A' MINOR are 'scale buddies'.
They share the same key signature.

The Key Signature of Scarborough Fair shows that there are no sharps or flats.
This would usually indicate that the piece has been written in the key of C major.
However, if you play the piece you will hear that it is in a MINOR key.

Play the scale of C major:

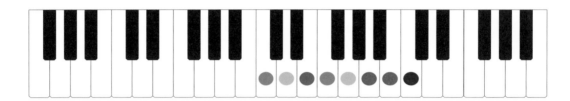

Now begin two steps lower on A.
The scale now sounds minor:

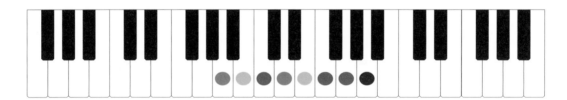

Very often the 7th note of a minor scale is raised (becomes a sharp).
Play this and listen to how this changes the sound.

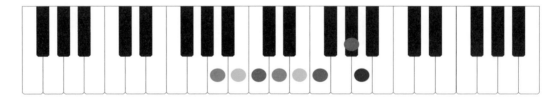

But this additional sharp **never** appears in the key signature.
It will appear in the music when it is required.

All major scales have a minor 'scale buddy' that
begins two notes lower and
shares the same key signature.
What is the minor buddy of

F major _____

Scarborough Fair

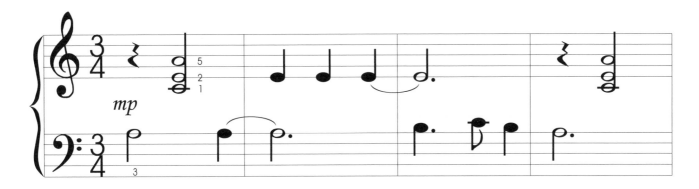

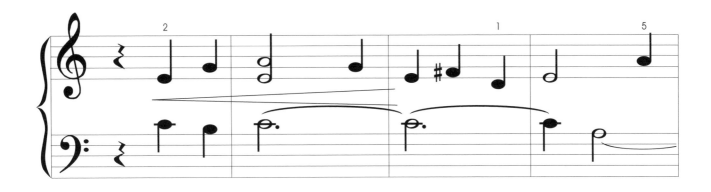

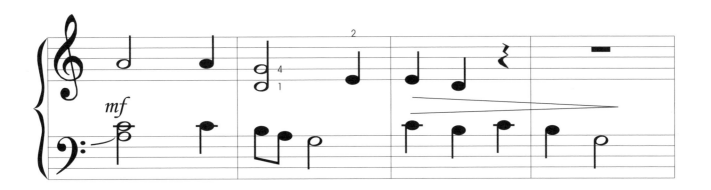

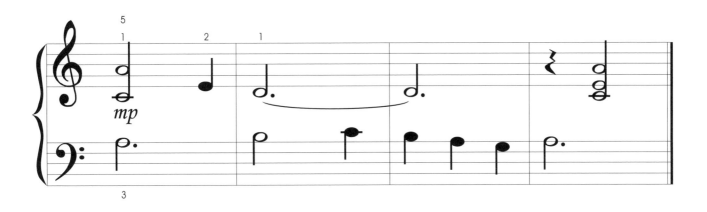

Compound Time

When we play in $\frac{6}{8}$ time the quavers are grouped together in threes.

This gives the music a different kind of rhythm.
It generallly makes the music feel as if it is *swaying* or *skipping*.

Draw lines between pairs of circles
that have the same value.

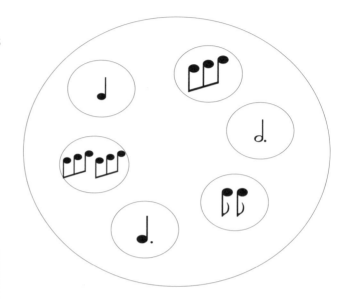

Practise your sight-reading by
playing this with each hand separately.
When playing with both hands
it may help to write in some
finger numbers.

Swimming With Dolphins

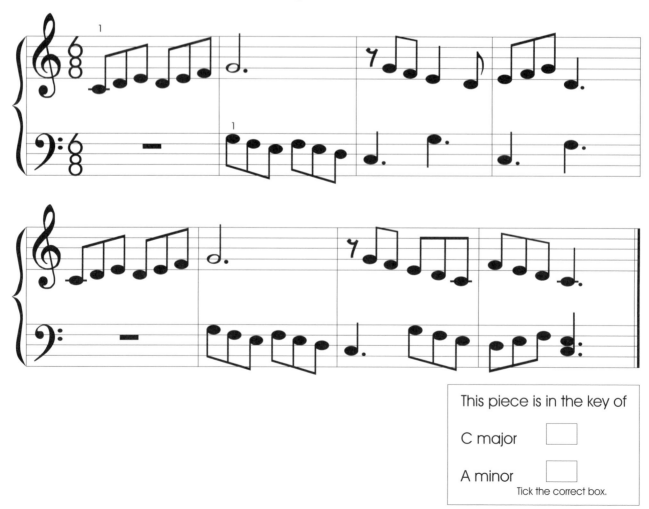

This piece is in the key of

C major ☐

A minor ☐

Tick the correct box.

Greensleeves

This piece is in the key of

C major ☐

A minor ☐

Tick the correct box.

Andante : walking pace

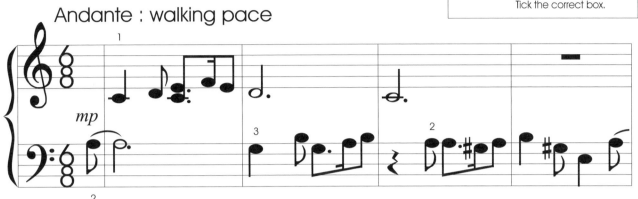

mp

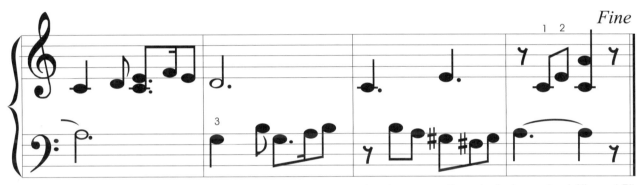

Fine

minor keys sometimes include a raised 6th and 7th.

Da capo al fine

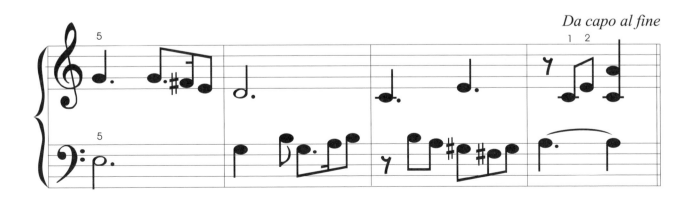

THE KEY OF D MINOR

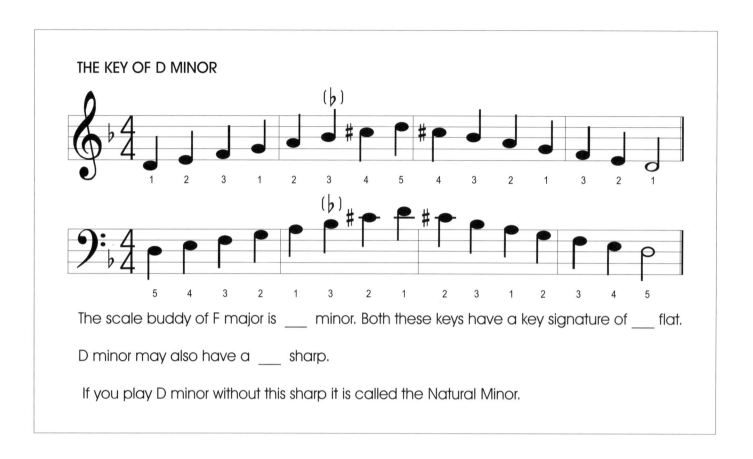

The scale buddy of F major is ___ minor. Both these keys have a key signature of ___ flat.

D minor may also have a ___ sharp.

If you play D minor without this sharp it is called the Natural Minor.

Funky Rabbit

Jazzy

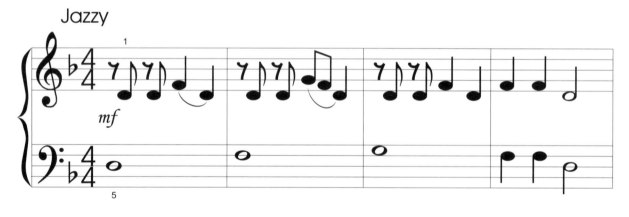

Bulldog Blues

Jazz style music very often uses a mixture of
major and minor and is more likely
NOT to include the extra sharpened 7th.

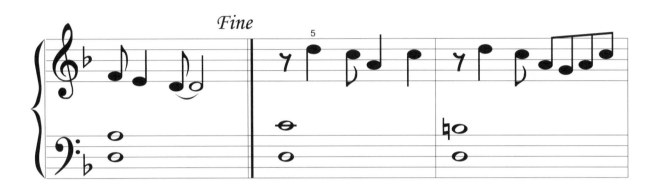

Fine

Da capo al fine

What interval is
played by the left hand
in the last bar?

3rd ☐

5th ☐

Tick the correct box.

Sometimes **quavers (quarter notes)** are grouped together.

Sometimes **quavers (quarter notes)** are on their own.

How many **quavers (quarter notes)** can you find in Bulldog Blues?

_____

The **time signature**
of Bulldog Blues tells us there are:-

Three crotchet beats (quarter notes)
in a bar ☐

Four quaver beats (eighth notes)
in a bar ☐

Four crotchet beats (quarter notes)
in a bar ☐

Tick the correct box.

Stormy Seas

Allegretto : fairly fast and lively

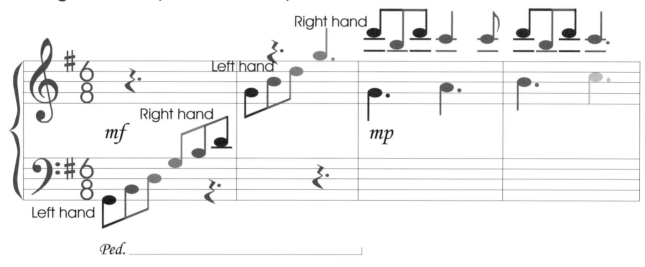

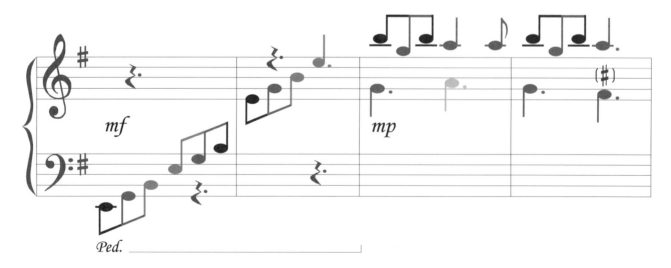

Which minor key shares its key signature with this major key? _____

In which bar does the key change to the minor? _____

Name the key:

The Hippo's Dream

Largo : slow and dignified

Activity Page

$\frac{4}{4}$ tells us there are ____ crotchet beats (quarter notes) in a bar.

$\frac{7}{4}$ tells us there are ____ crotchet beats (quarter notes) in a bar.

Write the names of the following notes.

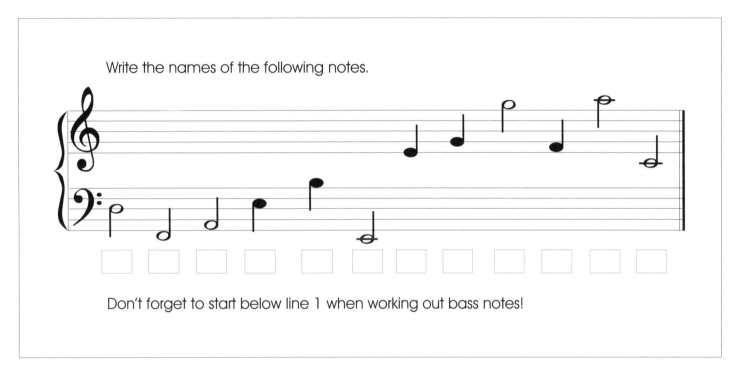

Don't forget to start below line 1 when working out bass notes!

Only 2 of these notes are Middle C.
Draw a circle around each Middle C.

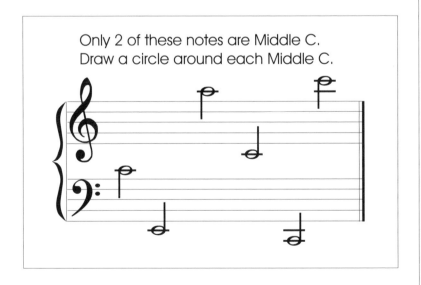

In the Hippo's Dream the interval played by the right hand in bar 1 is:

_____

The interval played by the right hand in bar 5 is:

_____

The interval played by the right hand in bar 6 is:

_____

The interval played by the left hand throughout the piece is:

_____

Name the key:

Toko's Boogie

Chinese Take-Away

Allegretto : fairly fast and lively

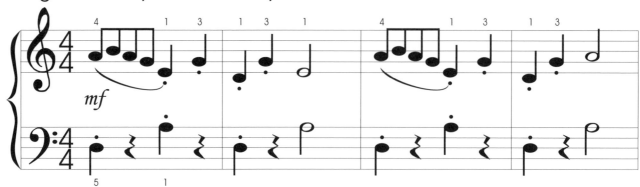

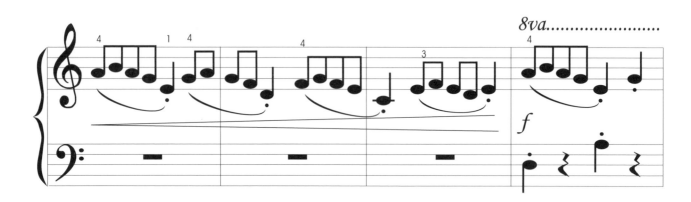

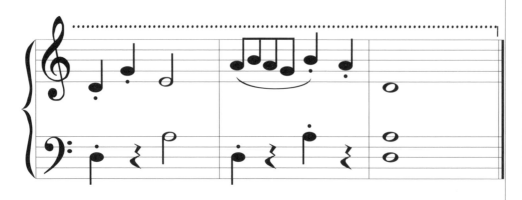

Not all music is written in major or minor keys. Listen to the sound of this piece.
It sounds minor but if it was in D minor it would have a B flat.
Music from other parts of the world often follow different scale patterns.

Name the key:

Russian Folk Song

Ludwig van Beethoven
1770 - 1827

Vivace : full of energy

Name the key:

Quadrille

Joseph Haydn
1732 - 1809

Allegretto : fairly fast and lively

Name the key:

A Little Dance

Czerny
1791 - 1857

Allegretto : fairly fast and lively

Name the key:

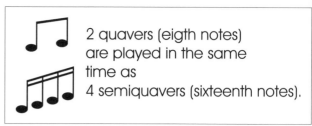

Ecossaise

This piece was written by Mozart when he was 8 years old
during a visit to London.

Mozart
1756 -1791

Allegretto : fairly fast and lively